Liquid Prayer
and Other Poems

Books by Butterfly Thomas

Head Held High (Urban thriller)
In My Feelings (Poetry collection)
The Butterfly Effect (Poetry collection)
Liquid Prayer (Poetry collection)

Liquid Prayer and Other Poems

From Hurt to Hope
in Three Acts

Butterfly Thomas

Independently published

Editing, print layout, e-book conversion,
and cover design by DLD Books
Editing and Self-Publishing Services

DLD Books

www.dldbooks.com

ISBN: 9798429922607

Dedication

This book right here, people,
This book right here, people,
Is dedicated to the Anita, to my Edward, or vice versa.
Also, in loving memory of Cliff and Claire.
No, not that Cliff and Claire.
#IfYouKnowYouKnow

Contents

ACT III: Hope

Kaleidoscope

What's my definition of kaleidoscope?
Something that spans the spectrum from despair to hope
A collage of colors and images to see
A hint, an impression of what could be
A smattering of shattered memories
A choking sorrow, so gripping, so deep
An enormity of emotion that brings you to weep
And everything that may fall in between

ACT I: Hurt

I'm going down
I can't stop crying, these tears keep on falling

Haiku 6

I love him deeply
now I miss him so fiercely
I weep profusely

Broken II

I knew you were hurt
I saw your pain
But you were inert
Wouldn't be moved
You didn't believe
Your situation would improve
Or couldn't believe
Whichever works for you?
Still I tried to help you gain
Your equilibrium
Your sense of self
You pulled me in
You pushed me out
You didn't need my help
I knew…
God was there… as I was
And I knew…
I knew what ending a marriage does
I knew the destruction, the devastation
I knew the reconstruction, the re–creation
The trying to make sense of the nonsensical
The reframing in your head, the overthinking
The self–blaming, the recriminations, the sinking…
Feeling that it's all your fault
Even though it's not
I knew you weren't healed
Aren't

I saw it clearly
I saw your exhaustion
I knew you were weary
Still I'm here... as God is
Quietly supportive of you
And whatever you endeavor to do
Because I knew
I know
I know the burden of dreams in flames
The sting of desires unquenched
I know not okay goes by different names
The suppression of emotions clenched
I know the feeling of losing everything
To have to again start over
I know what it's like to be lost yet determined
Bleary–eyed, but sober
God is here... as am I
When you're fine and when you're depressed
I know this, I know you, you can't hide
This is a journey, a nonlinear process
And this too, I know
I know a lot of stuff
Too much, not enough
Not the most important part
If only
I wish I knew...
How to unbreak your heart

New Direction

I sense a disconnection
A change in direction
From you
How do I continue to operate
It's too difficult to navigate
It's too new
Is this a wrong turn
Will we return
To us
A return to never
'Cause we never were
A return to almost
A return to pretend…
Nope, a dead end
A return to just friends
'Cause that's all we've ever been

Hurt Actually

Every day they come
Hot and unwanted
I push them back
But some days...
Some days they're undaunted
Like a river they flow
Burning, carving a track
Down my cheeks, around my nose
I don't like this feeling, alone
Where... are... you?
I pray without ceasing, I plead and moan, what did I do
Too many words left unspoken
Why did you go away?
Now I'm coping with a heart that's broken
Why didn't you stay?

Candy-Coated

Don't be fooled by the candy-coated exterior
Shiny and hard
It's my armor
Sweet and unassuming
It's my cover
Don't let the exterior
Lure you
Into a false sense of security
Like it's all good
Like I am
Because inside...
Under all of that...
I'm not
I'm not good
I'm not okay
My mind is all over the place
Tempting me to do stuff
Telling me I'm not enough
Lying...
Until I start crying
Doing too much
Saying too much
Not enough
I lost track
I just wanna black out
So I can't feel
What I'm feeling right now

Inadequate
Don't be fooled by the outside
Because inside?
When you scrape it away...
I'm not okay
I'm a mess

Cloud 9

Can I
Get high
Just to cope
With no hope
I want to float away
For the rest of the day
So I won't think about tomorrow
I drown my sorrows
The collapse of devotion
A tempest of emotions
I can't deal
Don't know how to heal
Poppin' not stoppin'
Smoking and choking
Drinking not thinking
Lying and crying
Trying to survive
To be revived
I need to get lifted
I mean, lift my spirits

Muddled Emotion

How do I feel right now?
Not sure
A mix of emotions I can't explain
Describe
Express
Reveal?
How do I say this?
What do I feel?
Do I want to
Cry
Scream
Rage
Smile
Laugh?
What is this?
I don't know
Melancholy
More like a tumbled jumble of emotions
A cocktail
Unmoored
Out of sorts
Off kilter
Unsettled

April Fools

Fool me once
Shame on you
Fool me twice
You know I knew
Fool me three times
Now I know what to do
Explore my free time
'Cause this ain't cool
Expand my me time
Tired of being April's fool
Focus on my purpose
Build my knowledge base
Do I still hurt, yes
So I put on a brave face
I go through each day
With a laugh and a smile
But I'm not okay
And I'm wondering how…
How how how
But I refuse to dwell on that anymore
I'm 'bout to show you what I got in store
I'ma take these emotions and use 'em as fuel
I'ma keep countin' blessings, keep collecting tools
Keep on learning as I'm going through
And I'ma stop being one of April's fools

Over You

Most days
I feel like I'm over it
I make myself believe it
I force myself
But then
There are the days between the good days
The days I realize…
That I'm just fooling myself
That I've not worked all the way through
That I'm not quite over it
Over you…

On a Memory

Sometimes when I think back
When I remember
When I reminisce
I wanna cry so hard
So bad
But I hold back
Even when I'm alone
I try not to let myself feel
All the feels
The glad
The mad
The sad
The memories, blissful
The could have beens, wistful
But they burn at the corners
Blazing
Scorching
Remnants of my pain
Held back
Yet somehow they still remain
Then they fall anyway

S&D (Samson & Delilah)

I know what this is…
Complete Frustration
At the powerlessness
In regard to this situation
Emotions entangled
And wrapped tight like thick strands
Yet once shorn away
It's out of your hands
You know who you are
But not what you want
You dismissed me easily
Now you act nonchalant
Oppositely
The grief won't control me
I know what to think
I know how to be
So I dismantle my braids
And take back my power
Add colored streaks
Or shear it in the shower
Here's what I think
As I restyle my short tresses
My emotions belong to me
I'm grateful for my blessins
So now I've rediscovered
Something I knew all along
Me cutting my hair
Is a new kind of strong

No Room

Is there still room for me?
Your friend, your besty?
When he finds she
Is there room for me?
After you marry
Will you still see me?
Can we chill?
Or will it be too chilly?
Cold shouldery?
I feel a little screamy
A little like a crybaby
Will you forget about me?
Our comradery
Is there still room for me?
I can't tell
Can't say
Can't do
How do I feel?
A little unglued
I got an attitude
I'm not in the mood
For this conversation
A separation
Of sorts...
Is there still room for me?
Will there be?
After...

Insufficient

How dare you
Not be enough
Unexpectedly
Catching me off guard
Causing me to have to re…
Recalculate, reorganize, recalibrate, redo, rewind
In my mind
My original plans
To adjust to new demands
But I refuse your insufficiency
Instead I speak abundancy
More than enough
A surplus
Not just of stuff
All needs met
All obligations kept
I know who got me
I know who's for me
I know who holds me
Can't none oppose me

ACT II: Healing

BS
I got this, I'm fixing my crown... You're not allowed

Mood Unknown

So, I'm in a mood today
I don't know what mood it is
Or why I feel this way

Contemplation

I sit and think what my life would be without you in it
Because I'm tired of the situation and I want to be rid of it
I wonder if I could do it myself and I think
Yeah I can
I can survive by myself
I don't need a man
For so long I have been waitin'
I just get excuses and lies
So guess what, I don't want you, yup
I've changed my mind
I've cried my last tear
The river in my soul has run dry
So there's nothing left to say to you
Except these words, goodbye
Or at least that's how I feel sometimes
When I'm sitting at home waitin'
Maybe someday I'll say those words
But for now I'm just contemplatin'

Release

Emotional ebb and flow
Happiness dipping low
Hurt and pain rising slow
Threatening to overflow
Carving each cutting blow
I feel it, figure 8 cycling from my head through my toes
But yet and still, I don't know
What I needed to show
What area did I fail to grow?
What did I do to make you go?
Or was it you?
What did you do?
To loosen the glue
Of what held us true
What grievances accrued
That made me lose
My peace
I can't cope with this grief
I need to release

Rhythm & Blues

You want my rhythm
But not my blues
Not the struggle to get out of bed
Not the day–to–day pain
Not the hurts left unsaid
Not the constant mental strain
You want my rhythm
But not my blues
The things I have withheld
You don't have a clue
So you feel a way
And lash out
With the things you say
A stab to the heart
To make your point
Destruction as you depart
You want my rhythm
But not my blues
I am not this pain
There is more in me
I'm not just these aches
Why can't you see?
I am still me
I still have feelings
You forgot my rhythm
And who I am
You forgot my joy

You don't understand
You forgot about the family
And what we vowed
You forgot for better or for worse
Only thought about for now
You forgot through sickness and in health
You forgot everything but yourself
You forgot about love
You forgot about us
Because my rhythm wasn't enough
And my blues had you stuck

Empty

Please explain this emptiness
There's something missing between us
Nothing's like it used to be
There are things we should discuss

                I'm empty

Sometimes it seems like you can't hear
But my words have power I'm certain
If I say it in this tone maybe you'll listen
And try to relieve this burden

                Fill me

We never do anything together
Do you have time for me?
Are you still in this relationship?
Not that I can see

                Fill me

I feel so unappreciated
I need my spirits to lift
You know what would make me feel better?
A simple thoughtful gift

                Fill me

You expect me to do this specific thing
But I just don't care to
Sure it's a quick and easy task
But it's something I don't do

                Fill Me

You never hug me anymore
I'm feeling a lack of affection

A squeeze or touch as you're passing by
I'm not asking for perfection
                              Fill me
This is what I need from you
And I guess you need some things too
Speak life into me with affirming words
If you do this, you will be heard
We should be making lifelong memories
I need quality time, can you hear my pleas?
This is what it takes for me
Give me a gift and I'll know you see
Do you respect me, your actions tell me no
If you do, acts of service would show me so
It seems you don't love me as much
Don't tell me, show me through physical touch
I must figure out how to meet your needs
And you must do the same for me
Love me, feel me, fill me,
So that my tank is not on E

Honestly

Honestly
Your dishonesty
Sickens me
Where is your accountability?
How can you say such things to me?
Do you have integrity?
Sense of responsibility?
Or are you just flagrantly
Skating by on apologies
Placating words you don't even mean
Honestly
Your dishonesty
Sickens me
You are not trustworthy
You have no dependability
Why are you trying to be
A part of this entity?
You don't deserve to be
Because you aren't a friend to me
When will you begin to see
Your deceiving ways aren't fooling me
You lack accountability
Your dishonesty
It sickens me
Honestly

Love is Blind

Something is wrong with you
Not with me
If that is all you see
My disability
There's so much more to me
So many different levels of intimacy
That we could reach
If you open your mind to possibility
Not just one aspect of me
I have plenty
A cornucopia to explore
But your myopia will have you ignore
An opportunity for more
To expand to grow
To uncover or discover
A new realm
So vast so wide
You can't help but step inside
And fall
Into an abyss
So wide so vast
Your love has come at last
Or will she be missed
Because of one little twist
You couldn't see... past this
Facet of me
And so you will be

Adrift in the sea
What a pity
A loss
A waste
Because in your haste
To dismiss who I was
Who I am
Who I'll be
'Cause of one part of me
You lost your chance
For an epic romance
Due to your decision
Based on your lack of vision
Your inability to see
All of me

Ex–Lover's Lament

(To the tune of "You'll Be Back": *Hamilton*)

You say
That you're still in love
Yet your actions don't seem to portray
You tryyyy
To pull me in a fool a–gain I just say hi
Oh you big mad
Remember the hate you sprayed when you went away
Now you making me laugh
Remember we are estranged you are not my man
I won't be back
Soon you'll see
You'll remember that I'm healing me
I won't be back
Time will tell
You'll remember you were treated well
Tempers rise
Boundaries fall
We have put each other through it all
Then I got a sign from above
We weren't an equal match so you don't deserve my love
Da da da da da

Yonely

Yeah my yoni is lonely
But not me
Oh no not me
Sometimes she fills with tears
But no one is there to wipe them away
Sometimes she wanna start talking mess
But nobody's there to hear what she gotta say
Yeah my yoni is lonely
But not me
Oh no not me
She's ready for a few things now
She's ready for adventure... she's ready for fun
She's ready to sing out loud
She's ready for a relationship... she's ready for the one
Yeah my yoni is lonely
But not me
Oh no not me
My yoni is different these days
She learned some stuff
The balance is better these days
She can be pliant... or tough
Yeah my yoni is lonely
But not me
Oh no not me
My yoni waiting on him
You know who I mean
They say good things come to those who wait

This remains to be seen
Yeah my yoni, she lonely
But not me
Oh no not me
Yesterday she cried
But today she okay
She hold it all inside
To be released when she pray
Yeah my yoni, she lonely
But not me
Oh no not me
Did I tell you she's over it?
Tired of being frustrated
She's eager for forever
She wants to be celebrated
She's a little anxious
But the time is right
She ready for him to find her
It's time to unite
But my yoni
Yeah she lonely
But not me
Oh no...
Not me

Phoenix

I'm flexing on my ...
Ashes
Not my ex's
'Cause like a phoenix
I rise
To compete with my new self
Not anybody else
Who knew?
That a change was due
A complete evolution
Such a simple solution
To the pain once felt
From the hand life dealt
I'm flexing on my...
Ashes
Not my ex's
Because the old me is dead
I got a new attitude
Forget what the past said
Watch what I do
I'm flexing on my...
Ashes
Not my ex's
'Cause like a phoenix
I rise
I won't die
I'm cut from a different cloth

I ain't built like that
I'm hard and I'm soft
I'm open and I'm closed
Who knows
Where I'm at?
Or where I'm coming from
I'm flexing on my...
Ashes
Not my ex's
This time around
Life's different I've found
I'm hip to the game
I don't move the same
'Cause we all make mistakes
It's part of the breaks
Lessons hard won
Experiences I needed
To exceed my comfort zone
To know I've succeeded
So, I'm flexing on my...
Ashes
Not my ex's
'Cause like a phoenix...
I rise

ACT III: Hope

Share my life
You are everything, what I need and all I want

Haiku 7

My pure hope will spring
Eternally like a star
That shoots through the sky

The End

I'm only 35, 45, 55...
I'm not ready to die
With fear trying to paralyze
Dreams half realized
I'm ready to thrive
Not just survive
I'm ready to make my presence known
Make my mark
Shoot my shot
Go big or go home
I still got so much life to live
So much love to give
I'm not done yet
This is only the beginning
Not the last inning
I have too much to do
To gain
To give
To learn
To build
To pour
To win
This ain't the end

Liquid Prayer

I cry out to you oh Lord
My needs, a slow trickle of salt
Spilling out fat heavy drops, my purpose caught
A call
Obligations big and small, a steady stream
The increase
A river of hopes, of dreams
My desire though
My desire for love so great it sweeps
So deep
An ocean covering my cheeks
I cry out to you oh Lord
Every tear
A liquid prayer
Then I wonder…
Do you hear?
Are you there?

Ready

Lord bring my husband to me
I'm ready for him to converse with me
Lord bring my husband to me
I'm ready for courtship and company
Lord bring my husband to me
I'm ready for love to encompass me
Lord bring my husband to me
I'm ready for all types of intimacy
Lord bring my husband to me
I'm ready to feel his arms around me
Lord bring my husband to me
I'm ready for us to meet each other's needs
Lord bring my husband to me
I'm ready for him spiritually
Lord bring my husband to me
I'm ready for soul rock consistently
Lord...
I'm ready...

Partner Prayer

Lord bring him to me
My partner to be
The husband for me
Speak to me intellectually
Captivate me mentally
Engage with me humorously
And also afro centrically
First level of intimacy
Match me spiritually
Walk with me and He
Faithfully
I will submit to thee
Lead me respectfully
Second level of intimacy
Be affectionate with me
Show me love physically
Comfortably
Hug me and squeeze me
Touchy feely
Third level of intimacy
Share your emotions with me
Understand me deeply
Let's explore each other fully
Display your honesty
Reveal your vulnerability
Feel me
Fourth level of intimacy

Come with me
To a new city
Visit with me
An African country
Dream with me
Create lasting memories
Experientially
Fifth level of intimacy
Seek me
Find me
For I am ready
To walk into my new life
With you my husband and me your wife
Of these things I speak life
And so they will be
As I decree...
Amen

Sweet Seduction

Let me...
Capture your attention
Entice your curiosity
Seduce thee
Inspire your imagination
Explore your verbosity
Let me
Captivate your senses
Counter your witty repartee
Seduce thee
Defeat your defenses
With the characteristics I display
Let me
Intrigue your thoughts
Reveal your subtleties
Seduce thee
Your secrets caught
Your love held close to me
Let me
With the nuances in my mind
Seduce thee
Take a peek and you will find
An abyss

Unaware

I love us talking every day
I love the witty things you say
I didn't know I'd ever feel this way
Open and brave
Like a brand new day
More myself
In a way
In a word
Or three
I'm more me
Stronger from knowing you
Enhanced
Blessed for growing through
This expanse
Of time
With you
Who knew?
Not me
Not you
Apparently
We were due
For this interlude
Caught off guard
And unaware
For this season
Of building and receivin'

Crush (Reprised)

I really like you and I can't deny
I'm falling for you and my feelings can't hide
I'm trying to grasp the meaning of this
The reason I get chills when we kiss
My emotions are starting to deepen, to grow
So there's one little thing I want you to know
Well, I guess by now you must
Be able to tell I have a crush
And so suddenly you're no longer reticent
So many things becoming evident
The way you feel about me… and I about you
'Cause honey I know you have a crush too
There's an opportunity here for more
I'll cherish you and you'll adore
Me
And we
Will, we can
Grow together
Hand in hand
Sharing our lives
Till the end of time

Ride the Beat

Eyes half–lidded, peeking
Together in our pleasure seeking
                    He loves
How my hips roll up slow
And rock down low
                    The Way
I take him inside
Our cores collide
                    I ride

A sensual slide
Up and around
I clench and release
Pulse and squeeze
To
                    The Beat
The rhythm, it feeds
My desire for him
His need for me
For my heat
To consume him
A union
Soul fusion

Strumming

Chocolate fingers stroking taut strings
Strumming
Humming the melody it brings
Just learning by touch, by feel, by sound, by hear
Just playing around, the sounds drawing you near
Chocolate fingers stroke up the neck and down around the
    base
Strumming
Humming with the rhythm it makes
Unaware of proper keys, techniques, just doing what I do
Capturing your full attention, while I play a song for you
Chocolate fingers stroking...
Strumming...
Humming...

Ready (Part 2)

Oh I'm ready
My entire body aching
For the absolution of touch
It's time for soul shaking
For adrenalin's rush
The feather–light tickle of roaming fingertips
The sensual caress of lips on lips
On nipples
On hips
The squeeeeeeze of steel of velvet in pulsing grips
The feel of your lingua as it twirls and dips
Sips
Then you slip in
Slide
Glide in
Dive in
Thrive in
Side
Then together
We come apart
Oooh I can't take it
Too much sensation
And still I crave it
Crave you
My boo

Kismet

Destiny divine
Yours and mine
Cosmically entwined
Flames twinning
Uncannily similar
Eerily familiar
Universe winning
Known in another life
You and I
My husband, your wife
Emotions spinning
Drawn to me
A pull of something deep
Drawn to you
A pull of something true
Is it fate?
For us to date
To marry
To carry
A love that's kismet
A slight hint
It's written
A blueprint
A chance
For our twin flames to dance
In unison
Together as one
Stronger, greater than the sum

Can You Tell

The words he says to me are
Bouquets of roses... or chocolate
When he's in the next room I
Miss him like crazy
When he's with me I'm falling
All over myself to do for him
When he sleeps I listen to
Him breathe
And I smile to myself
It's the little things
Can you tell...?
I'm in love

Make Me Better

There's a deeper love
Insida me
When we
Get together
Cuz you
Inspire
Me
To do better
To reach higher
We motivate each other
To elevate others
To vibrate higher
To come out of the mire
A singular movement
But together we're a force
Together we change the course
The way
The direction
With gentle correction
Cleansing fire
For the thoughts and the spirit
To cleanse those who get near it
And after we do
What we need to
To help others
We come back to
Ourselves to help us

As people tend to
Do
And privately
I come to you
Intimately
You claim me
Primally
Oooh bay bee
I crave thee
Then we
When we
Come together
We become better
True
A singular movement
But we're a force when we're together
Just us two

About the Author

Butterfly Thomas was born in Germany to two military parents but was raised in Virginia, where she still lives. When she is not working her day job as a counselor and advocate, she spends her time with the two loves of her life, reading and creative writing. She is a lifelong learner and tries to make time to watch *Jeopardy!* every night. She also admits to a hopeless addiction to chocolate.

Email: butterfly.m.enterprises@gmail.com
Website: https://www.dldbooks.com/bthomas/